ISBN-13: 978-1-7324900-6-2

Book Design and Illustrations by Uzuri Designs
www.uzuridesigns.com

Lil' Sass and The Adventure of Joy

Written by Christie Mann

Lil' Sass Explores her Emotions and Learns that it's OK to Express Joy and Happiness

Dedication & Acknowledgements

For all the little hearts in my life, watching you grow is one of my greatest joys, and it inspired me to write this series. And for your mothers and fathers–because without them, you would not be here and Sass would not have been birthed. Thank you!

For my healers, teachers and tribe. Sass was born from these classrooms and teachings and she is a portal through which I can spread these technologies and teachings. Ho! And So, it is! Sat Nam!

For my Pops, who reminds me that "Joy is not in things, it is in us!" I love you. Cape On!

For all of us who, at times, might be afraid to feel and express our emotions but move past the fear to allow ourselves to have the full range of our human experience.

Last, but not least, for the real Mrs. Moo: You may truly never know just how significant the positive impact your true friendship has had on my family and me. Thank you for letting me sit at your kitchen table and feel my emotions. I love you.

Cape On!

A Note to Parents and Caretakers:

I'm super excited for you and your kid(s) to meet Lil' Sass and accompany her on her adventures as she learns about her emotions. This topic of both having and being with our emotions isn't always an easy one. I learned this through my own journey, which is why I wanted to create Lil' Sass: to help adults and children talk about and experience emotions in a healthy, supportive way. I hope these stories support you as much as they support your child(ren). I share this with you with deep gratitude and respect for your dedication to your role as a parent and caretaker.

Cape On!

Sincerely,

Christie Mann

Meet Lil' Sass.

She is ten years old and is independent, clever, and determined. Her real name is Grace, but ever since she was a baby, her parents have called her Lil' Sass because she is just so adventurous and curious.

Lil' Sass lives in Venice Beach, California with her Mom. She likes roller-skating, going on adventures, and making new friends. Her dad used to live with them, but he and Mom started arguing a lot, and then he left. A few days after he left, her friend, Mrs. Moo, gave her The Red Cape.

Mrs. Moo is a kind and wise older lady who rents the little house in the backyard. Her job is to help people feel things. When she gave Lil' Sass The Red Cape, she said, "Sass, you can go inside of this Cape and feel whatever you are feeling. Just say, 'Cape On!' There, inside your Cape, you can explore and express all of your emotions."

"Feeling is a gift you give yourself. It is your right as a human being to experience your emotions— all of them." Emotion is the word Mrs. Moo uses to describe feelings like anger, sadness, and joy. As Sass goes about her adventures, she explores new emotions with her Cape.

The Adventure of Joy

It was a big day down at the roller rink!
Lots of local friends and tourists were enjoying
the blue sky and the bright shining sun
on the beach.

Sass skated straight by and into the roller rink
where she, Mr. O.G., and Tommy were going
to perform their skating routine in front
of an audience. Mr. O.G. was one of the "Original
Gangsters," a nickname his friends gave him
because he had been roller skating in Venice Beach
for so long. He was always so kind to Lil' Sass,
and taught her how to do dance routines
on her skates.

Tommy was Sass' best friend. He and Sass
had been working on this particular routine
for a long time! They skated around the rink
with Mr. O.G., shivering with nervous excitement
and energy while the crowd grew bigger
and bigger.

Then, Mr. O.G. pulled them aside to give them a pep talk before the performance began. "You have both practiced and worked hard for this day. No matter what happens, just enjoy your time out there. I know you are both so happy when you skate, so just let that joy and happiness come through you. That is really all that matters."

Mr. O.G. rubbed both of their heads and gave them the thumbs up as he skated away. Lil' Sass gave Tommy a high-five, and he gave her a quick hug. Sass was feeling really good! She realized that she was feeling joy!

Lil' Sass wanted to yell, **"Woohoo!"** and do cartwheels on her skates.

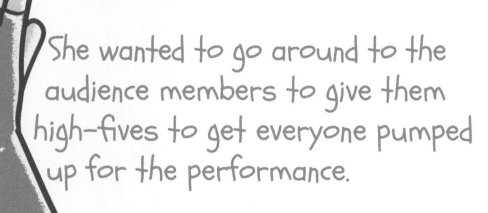

She wanted to go around to the audience members to give them high-fives to get everyone pumped up for the performance.

Instead, she stopped in her tracks,
unable to say or do anything! Instead,
she thought about all the things people had told
her about feeling happy and expressing her joy.

There was the time Sass won a poetry performance contest. She had been asked to perform her poetry again at school.

Sass' grandma stopped her and said, "Now Sass, this is great news, but you do not want to jinx this next performance by being so excited or over-confident. Do you know what I mean by 'jinx'? It means it is better to stay calm and to keep your joy to a minimum for now to ensure you do not ruin your chances for your upcoming performance."

Sass noticed the joy leave her body like air leaves a popped balloon. She decided to stay calm, so calm she stayed.

Then there was the birthday when she got the high-top roller skates that she wanted so badly.

She was spinning with excitement. Then Dad said, "Sass, shhhhhhh, calm down, you will make the other kids jealous. Remember, some of the kids do not have the money to buy these skates, so it is better to stay calm and not be too joyful about your gifts."

She did not really understand what Dad was saying, but he looked concerned. She asked herself, "How could my joy make others feel jealous? Wouldn't they be happy for me?"
She was confused, so she decided to stay calm, and calm she stayed.

Mr. O.G. tapped Sass on the shoulder.
"Sass, what's up? You're not moving."
Sass asked Mr. O.G., "Does feeling my joy jinx
things? If I show how excited and joyous
I am right now, will that make us mess
up the routine?"

"I do not think so," Mr. O.G. replied. "Some people
worry about jinxing because they want
to protect themselves from feeling let down.

Other times, people think that if you talk too much about the things that bring you joy, you are bragging. I disagree. I think that being excited about sharing our hard work and expressing our joy can only be a good thing!"

Sass relaxed and started to laugh. He was right! All this joy could not be bad. She knew in her heart that she wasn't showing off, but rather celebrating her hard work.

Lil' Sass thought back to what Mrs. Moo had said to her the day she gave her The Red Cape. "Sass, some days you will experience so much joy that you will want to spread the wings of your Cape and fly, so that you can spread the joy to everyone!

Do that. Do not ever dim your light! Your joy is contagious and will spark happiness and joy in others. Do not ever believe that it is wrong to be joyous or to feel this emotion, okay? Feeling this emotion is your right as a human being."

Mr. O.G., Tommy and Lil' Sass got into formation and began the routine. It was great! They were in line, they were on time, and the crowd loved it.

Sass took in the moment. She felt her own joy and the joy of all her friends.
They completed the routine and the audience clapped and cheered.

They chanted, "encore, encore, encore!"

Sass felt a bubbling sensation in her stomach, kind of like butterfly wings flapping. The flapping gave her an urge, and she decided to follow it.

"Cape On!" Sass spread her Cape wide and skated around the rink really fast with a great big grin on her face, saying, "Thank you, thank you, thank you!" Sass realized that she loved this feeling of joy, and wanted to celebrate it freely!

She thought about things her grandma and dad had said about expressing joy. She now knew that some of those things were not the same as what she was learning. The fact that Sass was enjoying this moment of celebration did not mean that she was rubbing her success in other people's faces or that she would jinx future performances. She was simply spreading more joy!

After the show, Lil' Sass saw a little girl who was learning to skate. Sass skated over to her. The girl said, "You guys are so inspiring! You are having so much fun that I want to learn, too! Thank you for sharing your joy."

Sass grabbed her hand and said, "Here, follow my feet! You can do this." Then she showed the girl some beginner dance steps, just like Mr. O.G. had showed her when she first started skating.

Lil' Sass wanted Mr. O.G. and Tommy to know it was okay for them to feel their JOY, too.

She cried, "Cape On!" and pulled them into the Red Cape with her.

Then she shouted,
"Ready, on the count of three,
put your hands up and yell JOY!
One, two, three, JOY!"

They threw their hands up in the air,
yelling "JOY!" as they laughed.

Discussion Guide

Cape On, Moms, Dads and Caretakers!

Lil' Sass is here to teach your kids about feeling their emotions all the way, and empowering them to do so with confidence. But she can't do it alone! As you read through Sass' adventures, please use the following questions to stimulate discussions with your kids about their emotions and their relationship with their emotions.

I encourage you to be open by revealing some of the toughest emotions you've experienced in a way that your kids can understand. Then invite them to do the same, and be ready to hold space and support whatever comes up for them. Feeling and experiencing our emotions is a lifelong journey, and together, we can help point kids along the way. Remember what Mrs. Moo says, "Feeling emotions is our right as human beings!"

Cape On!

Questions:

- Sass feels really joyful about her performance! Have you ever felt joyful about something you worked hard on?

- What else makes you feel joy?

- Sass gets a feeling of butterflies in her stomach when she is experiencing joy. What happens in your body? Where do you feel joy in your body?

- Did you ever feel jealous of another kid? If so, how did you handle that?

- Did you ever think another kid may be jealous of you? What was that like for you?

- Do you think there is such a thing as "jinxing"?

- What are you learning about emotions?

- What other emotions are you curious about?

READY TO CAPE ON?

Visit the Sass Shop to get a cape
for Mom, Dad, caretakers and kiddos!

FREE BONUSES!

Discover free bonuses for Lil' Sass readers!
Visit www.lilsass.com

EXPLORE MORE BOOKS
by Christie Mann

#CAPEON

About the Author

Christie Mann has made it her mission to be an 'ever-student' to fulfill her purpose of being a leader who develops leaders, who develop leaders. Christie is an author, spiritual psychologist, leadership coach, learning consultant, trainer, speaker and Kundalini Yoga & Meditation teacher who designs and facilitates transformational content and experiences that make our world a happier, healthier and more connected place to be.

At 13-years-old, Christie's life suddenly and dramatically shifted when she suffered some devastating losses and was thrust into a leadership position, which subsequently, impacted her relationship with her own emotional growth. She has spent the better part of the past two decades on her own corrective path and, because of this, has a sincere desire to encourage others to have a healthier and more responsible relationship with their emotions.

She is the creator of The Adventures of Lil' Sass, a series of personal development books for young people, accompanied by supporting accessories & experiences – a brand that teaches the importance and value of being with our own emotions and shows us how much JOY we can experience when we allow ourselves to be fully self-expressed. She draws inspiration for the characters, stories and accessories from her own life experiences and her learnings from Therapy, the Co-Active methodology through CTI, a Master's Degree in the Practices and Principles of Spiritual Psychology from the University of Santa Monica, and her practice of the ancient technology of Kundalini Yoga. Christie also obtained an Undergraduate-Degree in Media, Information and Technoculture from the University of Western Ontario.

Originally from a small town in Ontario, Canada, Christie now lives in Venice Beach, California where you can find her at the Venice Roller Rink, the sunny shores of the Santa Monica Pier or at RAMA, a local Kundalini Yoga studio. An Auntie many times over, she's in awe of children's resilience and emotional flexibility and champions adults' rights to have and express emotions too.

Cape On!

A Deeper Cut on the Dedication
& Acknowledgements

For all the little hearts in my life: Carson, Mia, Kingston, Cee Cee, Abbey, Will, Sebby, Hugo, Willow, Tommy, Jake, Lily, Brooks, Biba, Ma'ila, Rafi, Benji, Ellis, Althea, Alec, Mavis, Véronique, Freddy, Camille, Nik, Oliver, Luke, Gen, Gabby, Sophia, Reese, Tessa, Chloe, Mila, Jamie, Nathan, Noora & Israa. Watching you grow is one of my greatest joys, and it inspired me to write this series and create this brand. And for your mothers and fathers – because without them you would not be here and neither would Sass. And for D, for reigniting the spark of Sass in me – so she could be birthed.

Thank you to my dear friends, whom I call family. And to my dear family, whom I call friends.

For my healers, teachers and tribe. For Katherine Belfontaine for being the first one to make it safe to express my emotions—all of them. For Henry, Karen and Laura for birthing CTI/Co-Active and my Co-Active Family for creating experiences and circles where I am safe to go deeper and share more of my authentic self. For John: Thank you for your grace, equanimity and unconditional love. For my Purple Hearts, Teachers Ron and Mary Hulnick, and the practices and principles of Spiritual Psychology from USM. For Pam, thank you for helping me heal my body and introducing me to Melinda to heal on other planes. For Birch, you are a goddess and a magician. For Britta and Lee Eskey and the deep healing and courageous expression of ALL emotions through the COR experiences and brave community. For my community of Yogis and Teachers: Hawijian, Tej, Guru Jagat, Gurujas, Jai Gopal, Raghubir and the study and practice of Kundalini Yoga. Sass was born from these classrooms and she is a portal through which I can spread these technologies and teachings. Ho! And So, it is! Sat Nam!

For Pops, Momma and Stuy, I see you and I love you. Cape On!

For all of us who at times might be afraid to feel and express our emotions but, regardless, move past the fear to allow ourselves to truly have the full range of our human experience.

Last, but not least, for the real Mrs. Moo: You may truly never know just how significant the positive impact your true friendship has had on me and my family. Thank you for letting me sit at your kitchen table and feel my emotions. I love you.

Cape On!

CPSIA information can be obtained
at www.ICGtesting.com
Printed in the USA
BVHW02s2037040918
R9029900001B/R90299PG525872BVX1B/1/P